A Monster Truck's Day

by Rebecca Sabelko
Illustrated by Christos Skaltsas

BLASTOFF!
MISSIONS

BELLWETHER MEDIA
MINNEAPOLIS, MN

Blastoff! Missions takes you on a learning adventure! Colorful illustrations and exciting narratives highlight cool facts about our world and beyond. Read the mission goals and follow the narrative to gain knowledge, build reading skills, and have fun!

Traditional Nonfiction

Narrative Nonfiction

Blastoff! Universe

MISSION GOALS ▪ ▪ ▪ ▪ ▪ ▪

> FIND YOUR SIGHT WORDS IN THE BOOK.

> LEARN ABOUT THE DIFFERENT PARTS OF A MONSTER TRUCK'S DAY.

> LEARN ABOUT DIFFERENT TRICKS A MONSTER TRUCK CAN DO.

This edition first published in 2024 by Bellwether Media, Inc.

No part of this publication may be reproduced in whole or in part without written permission of the publisher. For information regarding permission, write to Bellwether Media, Inc., Attention: Permissions Department, 6012 Blue Circle Drive, Minnetonka, MN 55343.

Library of Congress Cataloging-in-Publication Data

Names: Sabelko, Rebecca, author.
Title: A monster truck's day / by Rebecca Sabelko.
Description: Minneapolis, MN : Bellwether Media, Inc., 2024. | Series: Blastoff! Missions: Machines at work | Includes bibliographical references and index. | Audience: Ages 5-8 | Audience: Grades 2-3 | Summary: "Vibrant illustrations accompany information about the daily activities of a monster truck. The narrative nonfiction text is intended for students in kindergarten through third grade."-- Provided by publisher.
Identifiers: LCCN 2023014280 (print) | LCCN 2023014281 (ebook) | ISBN 9798886873870 (library binding) | ISBN 9798886875256 (paperback) | ISBN 9798886875751 (ebook)
Subjects: LCSH: Monster trucks--Juvenile literature.
Classification: LCC TL230.5.M58 S23 2024 (print) | LCC TL230.5.M58 (ebook) | DDC 629.223/2--dc23/eng/20230329
LC record available at https://lccn.loc.gov/2023014280
LC ebook record available at https://lccn.loc.gov/2023014281

Editor: Christina Leaf   Designer: Andrea Schneider

Printed in the United States of America, North Mankato, MN.

This is **Blastoff Jimmy**! He is here to help you on your mission and share fun facts along the way!

Table of Contents

25

Ready for the Show!

The monster truck is getting **tuned up** for its big show.

The **crew** checks the **engine**. Now the truck is ready to show off for the crowd!

5

It is time to load the trailer. The crew removes the truck's huge tires. They put on smaller tires. The big tires will go back on at the track.

The truck rolls into the trailer. Time to go to the track!

tire

▶ JIMMY SAYS ◀
Monster truck tires are 66 inches (168 centimeters) tall. They are about the same height as most cars!

trailer

At the Track

At the track, the truck goes to the **pit party**. Fans line up to see the truck.

People take photos of the truck up close. They meet the driver.

driver

fans

It is almost showtime. The truck waits with the other trucks in the **hot pit**.

track

Soon, the driver steers the monster truck onto the track. Its engine roars for the crowd!

The monster truck's first event is a race. It lines up against another truck.

The driver **revs** the engine. The light flashes. Go!

The truck speeds down the track. It hits a jump and lands with an **endo**!

The front of the truck smashes into the ground. It cannot finish! The crew rushes out to see the damage.

jump

JIMMY SAYS

Monster trucks can travel more than 130 feet (40 meters) off a jump!

After a few repairs, the truck is ready for the **freestyle** event. It rams through a **wall of steel**!

wall of steel

Next, the truck spins. It does a **cyclone**!

The truck speeds off a ramp and does a **wheelie**.

wheelie

Then, the truck drives up a wall. Fans cheer as it does a backflip. The truck's tricks earn a high score!

On to the Next Show

After the show, the crew washes the truck. They make repairs and change its tires.

Soon, the monster truck is ready to rev its engine again!

Monster Truck Jobs

get tuned up

go to a pit party

race and do tricks at a monster truck show

Glossary

crew–a group of people who work on and make repairs to a monster truck

cyclone–a monster truck trick that involves quickly spinning the truck in circles in one spot

endo–a move when a monster truck rolls end over end

engine–a part of a monster truck that gives it power

freestyle–a monster truck event in which drivers perform tricks of their choice

hot pit–a place where monster trucks wait during monster truck shows

pit party–an event before a monster truck show where fans get to see monster trucks up close, meet drivers, and take photos

revs–turns a part of the engine; the engine makes a loud noise when it revs.

tuned up–fixed up and put into good shape

wall of steel–a wall of stacked cars that a monster truck smashes through

wheelie–a trick during which a monster truck stands straight up with the front wheels in the air

To Learn More

AT THE LIBRARY

Abdo, Kenny. *Monster Truck Rallies*. Minneapolis, Minn.: Abdo, 2019.

Adamson, Thomas K. *Monster Trucks*. Minneapolis, Minn.: Bellwether Media, 2019.

Arnold, Tedd. *Fly Guy Presents: Monster Trucks*. New York, N.Y.: Scholastic Inc., 2019.

ON THE WEB

FACTSURFER

Factsurfer.com gives you a safe, fun way to find more information.

1. Go to www.factsurfer.com.

2. Enter "monster trucks" into the search box and click $\mathcal{Q}$.

3. Select your book cover to see a list of related content.

BEYOND THE MISSION

> WHAT WAS THE MOST EXCITING PART OF THE BOOK TO YOU? WHY?

> WOULD YOU LIKE TO DRIVE A MONSTER TRUCK? WHY OR WHY NOT?

> DESIGN A MONSTER TRUCK. WHAT DOES IT LOOK LIKE? DRAW A PICTURE.

Index